tar heel born

CEDRIC BROWN

A NATIVE SON SPEAKS ON RACE, RELIGION, & RECONCILATION

Junie's Mood Press | Oakland, California | www.juniesmood.com

Tar Heel Born:
A Native Son Speaks on Race, Religion, & Reconciliation
(c) 2015 by Cedric Brown

All rights reserved. No part of this book may be reproduced or transmitted to any form or by any means without permission in writing from the publisher, except in case of reviews.

Published by:

Junie's Mood Press
PO Box 10095
Oakland, CA 94610
www.juniesmood.com

Book design and layout by Design Action Collective
Cover design by Kathy Azada

ISBN-13: 978-0-9857006-2-1
ISBN-10: 0985700629

Special thanks to:

My Ray of sunshine
Rebekah & Reggie
The Kapors (& their cottage)
Trevor & Oakstop
Melissa's eagle eyes
Archies, Alans, Browns, & a Douglas
Listening friends, Tar Heels & others:
   Andreana, Carmen C., Carolyn,
   Catherine, Charles, Cornelius,
   Derek, Joan, Joe,
   Lori, Parrish, Patrick,
   & Tilton

I'm a Tar Heel born
I'm a Tar Heel bred
And when I die
I'll be a Tar Heel dead

From the University of North Carolina Fight Song

I.

Give up on North Carolina?!

North Carolina loves me with
rich red clay earth
vibrant vernal tree canopies &
beige-sanded beaches gently rolling like
palms of God's outstretched hands
The color of the sky itself:
Carolina blue

North Carolina loves me through a sharp twang or smooth drawl
spoken with a practical sensibility
It loves me through Tobacco Road basketball &
rocking chairs & barbecue at the international airport
It loves me through heavy humidity like
body heat from being held close
"I'll pray for you" it says
& means it sincerely
most times

2012
I was chatting with a dear friend
a fellow Tar Heel & Son of the South
(so much so that his platinum-blonde hair
earned him the childhood nickname
Cotton)

Amendment One
banning marriage equality & civil unions
had just passed by a great majority in our home state,
North Carolina

Tar Heel Born
Cedric Brown

A vocal but outnumbered coalition of progressives
put up a vigorous fight
President Obama even weighed in saying
NO ON ONE
ultimately to no avail
The amendment became law

Cotton expressed his disgust with the outcome
of the Amendment One election:
I'M THROUGH WITH NORTH CAROLINA
I'VE HAD IT
& while I was also dismayed & deeply disappointed by the vote
my first reaction to his declaration was
GIVE UP on North Carolina?
Could we really ever DO that?
I pictured a sapling torn up from the ground
roots exposed & dangling
Can any of us really uproot what's deeply embedded
even as we live & work & perhaps
blossom
in other places?

That exclamation got me to thinking more about
my own conflicted relationship with North Carolina
This Tar Heel state
My home-away-from-home where the heart is
where beloved family, current & past, are anchored

I love North Carolina but
growing up there I was thrashing against
mainstream whiteness
mainstream heterosexism
To call myself an exile may be an inappropriate overstatement
But the feeling of living under imminent threat
of marginalization
of devaluation

Tar Heel Born
Cedric Brown

even of violent confrontation
is very real
& I
an odd aberration there
left to cultivate a life
& perhaps to save my own

This experience is certainly not unique to me
Others in my tribe & predicament
now an attorney in Philly
a businessman in San Diego
a professor in Chicago
a curator in San Francisco
a doctor without borders
et. al.
have left our Tar Heel birthland for warmer suns
unable to bear stunted growth in the state of home
leaving one to wonder what kind of effect
this outmigration wreaks on the state's brainpower & talent pool
Look what happened when John Coltrane
left
when Nina Simone
left
when Thelonious Monk
left
when Max Roach
left
Ernie Barnes
left
Roberta Flack
left
Romare Bearden
left
North Carolina-born brilliance
sprouted from outside the state line

Tar Heel Born
Cedric Brown

So I love North Carolina for birthing & raising me
& harbor some resentment for not embracing me
not making me feel safe enough to fully
blossom
within her boundaries

Tar Heel Born
Cedric Brown

II.
SCARS

Tar Heel Born
Cedric Brown

Deep running dark scars don't let me forget
Childhood was an extended lesson in
How to Not Be a Nigger
Scars, an appropriate metaphor
because while they don't hurt like the initial severing
the gashes don't disappear but
repair themselves as darker,
blacker in places

Scars from teenaged arrogance of peers
who knew
(or maybe just innately felt)
their superiority was assured because of white skin
Upturning noses at anything black
Recklessly wielding Nigger like a sword
alternately understanding & not understanding its tremendous power:
A disheveled whiteboy growling at fifth-grade-me
"Get out the way you little Nigger"
while I knelt to tie my shoe
A whitegirl telling me I'd Niggerized a pop song
by singing it with soulful riffs
A whitegirl naming her pet Nigger Kitty
"Not because it's a black cat," she said, "but because it's stupid"
A whiteboy equating his being left off the basketball team with
historical exclusion & economic oppression
(as a case of reverse racism, of course)
Whitekids defensively demanding why we didn't have
a white student union, a white cultural center
white entertainment teevee
Whiteboys repeatedly chanting
at a varsity game against cross-town rival Carver High
"watermelon watermelon
Cadillac car
we ain't as dumb as you think we is"

Tar Heel Born
Cedric Brown

I wish there was a statute of limitations on pain
to be wiped clean & clear from memory upon the expiration date,
not allowed to fester as epic baggage, carry-on or trunk-sized
But past hurts
however paper-cut small they may be now
are reminders of the trials of yesterday
So as much as I
well-adjusted, multi-therapied, & grown up
would love to forget them
I do remember
& those scars magnify
every bit of hate speech
(some thinly disguised as snark)
that I hear/read spewed today
My healthy suspicion & discomfort with white people
is rooted in gashes personal & impersonal:
Seeing American Nazi Party members
gun down demonstrators in Greensboro
& get off scot free
(by an all-white jury)
& remembering Ku Klux Klan memorabilia on display
at the local library
& witnessing recent gerrymandering & voter disenfranchisement
so clearly targeting black voters
resulting in the complete manipulation of a democratic political system
undergirded by fear & bigotry
How did we end up as unwanteds in this, our own land
which we should claim by birthright?

You're oversensitive
You're too race conscious
You can't take a joke
You're not like other black people so I can say it to you...

Tar Heel Born
Cedric Brown

One of the many benefits of
unexamined whiteness
is that whitefolks can move nearly unencumbered
without giving thought to race
except in rare
& usually negative
situations

These white peers had the luxury of not having to
interact with
converse with
ride the bus with
live near
play with
go out with
bond with
date
befriend
respect
or certainly not
LOVE
anyone Black

So even in the post-civil-rights-movement South
the children of the marchers
(among the first wave of integrators)
still were not free
to talk/think/walk/sing/dance
be
different
Under the eye-blistering glare of whiteness
anything dark became
inferior, less-than
Niggerized

Tar Heel Born
Cedric Brown

I still haven't figured out how to let go of the notion
that all whitefolks loathe
&/or are repelled by
all blackfolks
This prejudgement
rooted in scars
limits my own humanity
because I detest & resent the
people who (I believe) detest & resent me

To them we are Bigger Thomases
mugshots on the evening news
a vague & looming threat in dimness or daylight
To me they are
online trolls in OpEd comments sections
hiding (& sometimes not!) behind cyber anonymity
launching maddening screeds from every corner of the web
They are any/every member of the GOP
innovating new dog whistles for their
Southern Strategy-shaped base

The scarring has rendered me
unable to have genuine conversations with most Southern whitefolks
out of concern that their devaluation of blackness
inadvertent or innate
will catch me flatfooted & vulnerable
to the uppercut of edgy observations

Even whitefolk whom I love
& believe that they love me back as an equal
dear friends, beloved friends
have the Sisyphean task
(perhaps unknown to them)
of steadily proving their dedication to
progressive racial justice
But to what end?
All of it is exhausting

Tar Heel Born
Cedric Brown

I've tried to bury myself deep in the
liberal blue bubble of northern California
hoping to cushion from future gashes
wondering what would bring about full healing
Maybe the scars are too deep
& too often cut back open
So I pray that next generations find
the peace that I'm unable to have
as ghosts & doubts continue to jostle me
when sometimes I just want to rest &
trust that I'll be taken seriously as
a peer
an equal

a human

Tar Heel Born
Cedric Brown

Tar Heel Born
Cedric Brown

III.
FINDING GOD

Tar Heel Born
Cedric Brown

As a boy
I was continuously horrified at the prospect
of being perceived as girlish
So I did a lot of hiding around people
Even in plain sight I would try to hide:
Didn't want to talk with friends of the family
(& sometimes to family either)
Was uncomfortable in the presence of grown men
(thought they'd think I was a sissy)
Didn't wrestle rough & tumble games with other boys
but instead snuck to play with my sisters' dolls
Black Barbie had MUCH more fascinating stories to tell than
GI Joe or plastic army figurines
& she had better accessories, too

As much as I love blackfolks now
I used to hate being in (non-family) all-black environments
I couldn't breathe, had no space to be me
under the threats of name-calling & derisive laughter
I overheard occasional little comments about men being
"funny" & "shaky"
not having anything to do with humor or Parkinson's
I was told on occasion to
straighten my wrists &
never hold them limp
Take my hand off my hip
Walk straight; don't switch or swish
& don't cross my legs when I sit
In other words, do anything to stop being
a girly little boy
a little girly boy
"...a little girl, boy."

Tar Heel Born
Cedric Brown

Once a cousin called me a tomgirl
& she really didn't mean any harm
was only making a comparison
since I did like to jump rope & do arts & craftsy stuff
but I pinched her so hard for calling me a tomgirl
that she cried

From this difference
I developed an awareness
a shame, actually
well before age 12
when things took a decidedly hormonal turn

My big gay Aha moment
was in the summer before seventh grade
while looking at a classmate in the shower &
noticing his wonderful all-over teddy bear brownness
& feeling a quiet pleasure
almost like a sense of accomplishment
discovering a new definition of beauty
But of course I didn't share that with anybody
which unfortunately became my m.o. for dealing with desire:
notice but don't express it
don't tell anyone
shut your mouth
keep it to yourself
enjoy it by yourself
so no one else would know of your difference
your "deviance"

At the same time
throughout childhood generally
my siblings & I were being taught how to walk
a straight & narrow path
through year-round attendance at Sunday school & church
& Vacation Bible School in the summer

Tar Heel Born
Cedric Brown

To my young knowledge
everybody in our family & our extended family's families
believed in Jesus:
Prince of Peace, Rose of Sharon, Lily of the Valley, Lord & Savior
Ruler of our Lives

We weren't holy rollers but we were part of a lively congregation
complete with the requisite rollicking Baptist preaching
that built from a pastor's thoughtfully-considered observations
gaining locomotive-like momentum until it peaked at
passionate & punctuated declarations of truth & urgency
(most times shouted)
Because if the DOORS IN YOUR LIFE are CLOSED (ha)
it's JESUS (ha)
who will open 'em up (ha)
If the door is LOCKED
it's JESUS (ha)
who CARRIES THE KEY
It's MY LORD (ha)
who'll put SHOES on your feet so you can CROSS THE THRESHOLD
It's JE-EE-EE-SUUUUS
WHO MAKES A WAY OUT OF NO WAY

& the women would get the spirit & shout
cry, dance, stomp, lift hands & eyes to heaven
& sometimes even run up & down the aisles
Old deacons seldom did more than stood & pointed & acted as
the original hype men
to urge the minister on
Sometimes I wondered if the pastor would deem his sermon a failure
if nobody shouted or
nobody answered the call to be saved
to "give your life to Christ"
that followed every sermon, every Sunday

Tar Heel Born
Cedric Brown

Even then as a kid witnessing all of this
the performances were both mystical
& over the top, almost humorous
It wasn't until I was a teenager
& actually started listening to the sermon
that I at times became overwhelmed
by a spiritual welling-up of happiness & gratitude
of a bountiful & glorious thanks

I, too, wanted to shout out
but instead clamped my mouth shut
swallowed the exultation except for a few leaked tears

I thought I'd look & sound womanly
like some of the rather flamboyant men in the congregation
The quintessentially clichéd Church Queens
occupied the most space & air
in the choirs' tenor section
brought scarves & flair
to the usher board
& general panache to the Sunday proceedings

Our church had a gay cloud hanging over it anyway
Our pastor was rumored to have been in the midst of
sex with another man & got
"stuck"
inside the other man
(or vice versa, depending on who was spreading the rumor)
This tale was deemed true because a far-flung relative
or friend-of-a-friend-of-a-friend
witnessed the accused duo passing through the emergency room
still stuck in a most compromising position
The ridiculousness of it makes me mad even now
Both that fools would perpetuate this kind of rumor
AND that having a same sex liaison would be so deliciously scandalous
for so long

Tar Heel Born
Cedric Brown

The Church Queens were the first gay men I ever recognized
which was both comforting & unnerving
I looked at them as the extreme example of what I might become
Unsure what the quote unquote gay lifestyle would bring upon me:
Violence?
Loneliness?
Illicit, empty, unloved sex?
(Sneaking to read "The Sexual Outlaw" in the public library
surely didn't help me form a healthy perception)
I was clear that "the life" certainly would put me
squarely in harm's way
in the crosshairs of
relentless gossip & rebuke
slurs & rejection
Or so I thought
I was too afraid to associate with those men
who could've been mentors
so I held myself apart

Back in the day, "punk"
(pronounced "ponk"
out of black mouths)
was equated with "fag"
each spat out with abandon & precision
liberally & deliberately
I became an expert at dodging both the name-callers
& the words

As for religion
I never fully understood Christianity
Blood & crucifixion & Original Sin & all that
"Giving my life to Christ" made me think
I'd be a religious zombie
unable to enjoy any pleasure
Nose-deep in the Bible

Tar Heel Born
Cedric Brown

Did I believe
because of the power & truth
or because of Hell & damnation
(Who WOULDN'T be afraid?)
Church made me
humane & honest & gracious & grateful
propelling me with a sense of purpose & justice
& believing in a force greater than humanity
But I can't call it ever-nourishing
Sometimes I now miss the rituals & social circle
but certainly not the dogma

I don't remember anti-gay excoriations
from the pulpit of my home church
(not that it never happened)
Overt sexuality of any kind
(outside of the cover of marriage)
was generally taboo &
gayness was one of many sins to pray away
In the late 80s
the culture wars & AIDS crisis
brought anti-gay religiosity into razor-sharp focus
giving zealots a national platform to rail
against immorality & sin &
preach AIDS as God's vengeance:
a double-whammy cocktail of ignorant intolerance
so strong that some Church Queens succumbed to
self-doubt & self-rejection
backsliding into the closet

So while I don't embrace
that black folks are more "anti-gay" than other folks
much of it seems Christian-based
providing a penchant & purpose for vocalizing it
('Cause you know how loud we are)

Tar Heel Born
Cedric Brown

The prevalence of Christianity & churches
throughout the state
makes me wonder how we
Southern descendants of enslaved Africans
got to this place of
widespread religiosity
homogeneous thought
The Islam & Yoruba & Africanisms of our forbearers
beaten & brainwashed out of us
So with no other spiritual systems & religions
to contrast or challenge or complement or compare
(denominations don't count)
we swallowed Christianity & all that it brought
Built churches into bedrock community institutions
& divided life into saved & sinners
heaven-bound & heathens:
boxing us into other kinds of
overrestraint
teetotaling
"Black people don't..."
ski
travel
speak other languages
swim
camp
befriend whitefolks
eat vegetarian diets
& so on

I knew I had to get out of there
Where to think outside the Christian box is
at best a social demotion
at worst eternal damnation
even by folks you love

Tar Heel Born
Cedric Brown

When I hit California for the first time
sight unseen
I knew I'd found my Promised Land
where I could explore & grow & be supported
(& I don't mean experiment with drugs
become a nudist
or the other wacky things that people attribute to living in
pre-dot-com San Francisco)
I could grow locks & eat Asian food all week if I wanted
Practice French & play soccer if I wanted
Take Afro-Brazilian dance classes & learn the names of Orishas
if I wanted
Figure out how to embrace & love a man
if I wanted
& nobody blinked!

But not being a Christian isn't the same as embracing
agnosticism or atheism
I still believe in God as a power, a force
not diminished to traditional Christian interpretations
No matter what direction it blows
the wind is still the wind

It was only after I left church restrictiveness behind
that I found God in myself
(to borrow a line from Ms. Shange)
by embracing my truth & beauty
as one of the many forms that God presents as human
Gay
Me

Tar Heel Born
Cedric Brown

IV.
OF THE LAND

Tar Heel Born
Cedric Brown

I like the North Carolina kind of people
Down to Earth but reachin' for the moon
I like watching kids grow up/In a state of grace
On a North Carolina afternoon
Lord, it's just like living in a poem
I like calling North Carolina home•

If you've only experienced North Carolina
driving up the Eastern Seaboard via I-95
please
make no judgments from the repetitive blandness
of that 180-mile stretch
between the Virginia & South Carolina borders

The land, even just a stone's throw beyond the highway
is regally emerald & richly endowed

North Carolina has cradled all-comers
from the once ever-present indigenous
Catawba, Creek, Cherokee, Cheraw
to runaway enslaved Africans hiding in the Great Dismal Swamp
Her terrain was bloodied by rancor of warring white men
in Brunswick Town & Bentonville, Moore's Creek & Monroe's Cross
among other battlefields
Her land consecrated by settlers pursuing & creating new opportunities
over the centuries:
Europeans in the 18th
Freedmen in the 19th
Latin Americans in the 20th

Our North Carolina lessons began in the fourth grade
where I constructed a papier-mâché relief map of the state

* Jingle from 1970s tourism campaign

Tar Heel Born
Cedric Brown

Colored brown the Appalachians in the west
greened the rolling hills of the mid-state Piedmont region
chose a sandy yellow for the coastal plain next to
the royal blue fingers of the Atlantic
caressing the land

Our class learned about the state bird, the cardinal
& that to blow a kiss at a red cardinal
brings good luck
(a superstition I continue to practice)
We committed to memory the verse & chorus of our anthem
"The Old North State"
& how not everyone would cherish this place we lived but
our hearts swell with gladness
whenever we name her
(& mine still does)

All this was pretext for a four-day bus tour:
The North Carolina Trip!
I got new pajamas for the occasion
white polyester that fit snug like thermal underwear
a University of North Carolina Tar Heel logo
splayed across the chest

We traveled from the mountains to the sea
not quite from "Murphy to Manteo" as the saying goes
but hit a number of different highlights of
natural & national history:

The Blue Ridge Parkway, Blowing Rock &
Kerr Scott Dam
As a young Christian, I refused to say *dam*
even while understanding the difference
between the wall & the
expletive

Tar Heel Born
Cedric Brown

Upon seeing the Old Market House in Fayetteville
I was haunted by the knowledge that
enslaved Africans were once sold there
Wondering if my ancestors among them

At Fort Macon
The docent regaled us with tales of
Blackbeard's adventures & pillaging pirates
off that very coast!
That went over quite well with fourth grade boys

Fort Raleigh, Manteo
Site of lingering mystery
"Croatoan" carved into a tree
with no trace of the colony that once was there

Jockey's Ridge at Kill Devil Hills
From the tallest sand dunes on the East Coast
we marveled at the Memorial to a pair of intrepid brothers
who sailed through the air & changed everything,
forever

My wanderlust began on this trip:
The world was bigger than my hometown &
I wanted to explore that bigness

Even as a youngster
I knew & understood & loved
the state, the land, the legacy
as mine:
a citizen-owner

That love has perhaps mellowed or grown jaded over time
but as a Tar Heel by birth & bearing
I still feel like it's mine

*****

Tar Heel Born
Cedric Brown

North Carolina is tobacco country
historically the largest U.S. producer of the now-disgraced leaf
Nicotiana tabacum is woven throughout my maternal family history
From the fields to factory
forbearers picked, processed, & packaged it
R.J. Reynolds Tobacco Company provided stable work
for African American families
mostly through manual labor
& from those earnings, three waves of my family members
survived & thrived

Someday some of the land there will be mine
acquired as a debt of gratitude to my own/owned ancestors
in Chatham County
who tended farms & families under backbreaking conditions

Land will pay homage to my forbearers in Forsyth County
for the distance we've traveled in three, four, five generations
from harvest to higher ed.

Land earned by birthright
through hard work &
the heavy price of enslavement &
the exacting tolls of Jim Crow segregation & Reagan-era rollbacks

Land is a rite of passage into a bonafide adulthood
Despite other accomplishments
I feel I'm not truly grown until
my name is on a deed

Land is a stake in the ground
for generations to come
to never feel like an outsider
To declare "we own this & we belong here"
& be unshakeable in a confident citizenship
of the Good Ol' North State

Tar Heel Born
Cedric Brown

V.
CAROLINA, PRICELESS GEM

Tar Heel Born
Cedric Brown

I grew up surrounded by modesty
in a modest lower middle class family
in a modest lower middle class black neighborhood
in the modest city of Winston-Salem
A lovely place in many ways
green & pleasant in most parts
despite a lack of enticing natural attributes
like a slow-winding river sauntering through town or
mountainside vistas to gaze into far horizons
Tobacco was its claim to fame
The cigarettes
Salem & Winston
were named after the two towns
(& not vice versa):
Winston & Salem
which merged in 1913

There we lived a reasonably comfortable existence
certainly benefitting from quality teaching
a solid arts scene
& ever-present church circles
in addition to a large & loving extended family
well-known in the local black community
But there was no edge there
No Disney World thrills or big urban excitement or
Grand Canyon awe
I grew up missing something
dreamt of driving westbound on I-40
which ran through the heart of town
starting at the onramp near my elementary school & crossing
Tennessee, Arkansas, Oklahoma, Texas, New Mexico, Arizona
ending up in Barstow, California
I'd hoped to catch a glimpse there
of the Brady Bunch or the Bionic Woman
living lives of 1970s
Southern Californian outtasight-ness

Tar Heel Born
Cedric Brown

Closer to home
Chapel Hill was the laboratory where the alchemy of me
started to crystallize
It was love at first sight
on a springtime visit to the University campus
sprawling across the southern half of the town
like classy classroom kudzu
The dogwood trees greeted me with satiny fresh blooms
slightly pinked on their tender ends
waving through the Eastertime zephyr
& brick walkways & manicured quad lawns invited
Socratic-like contemplation of
lectures delivered by stodgy professors in starchy shirts
& a promise to indulge my sapiosexual tendencies
(not with the professors, to be clear)

So much of my North Carolina love is rooted at UNC
The University Of
No surprise considering the principle
Universitas
"a whole"
amasses a sum greater than its parts
Culling people from across the state
& aiming to unite them for the greater good
of the state & its people

My love affair with Carolina
(the University, as we Tar Heels call it)
was fast & deep &
like any marriage worth engaging in
had its ups & downs

Tar Heel Born
Cedric Brown

At Carolina
I
like those dogwoods
started to bloom
in the hothouse of the University
I felt creative
intelligent
experimental
outgoing & curious
less constrained
Meeting & befriending people
from throughout the state's nooks & crannies
Chinquapin & Cherokee &
Charlotte & Shallotte
Hickory & Hampstead
Wilmington & Washington
I got to know out-of-staters
New Jerseyans & New Yorkers
Virginians & Volunteers
Texans & Torontonians
& even a girl from Florida who had never seen snow
There we began to build bonds for a reason
a season, or in quite a few cases
a lifetime

At Carolina
We hung out at the Pit & on the Yard
waiting to see & be seen in that scene
even when we had more pressing things to do(!)

We thought globally & acted locally at the Campus Y
Built shantytowns to agitate for divestment from South Africa &
marched for a free-standing Black Cultural Center
Snuck snacks into the shiny new Davis Library for
late night cram sessions
(in a private study room if lucky)

Tar Heel Born
Cedric Brown

We bonded over basketball
& a burgeoning white hot rivalry with Duke:
a barely-concealed subtext of wealthy vs working class
Yanks vs Rebels
urban vs country
as the two teams traveled between campuses on
Tobacco Road

We treated ourselves to dinner & dates on Franklin Street
& lived in dinky apartments in Carrboro or
tiny rooms in South Campus highrises
& stood in long lines for class registration punchcards
& cabbage-patched into sweatered sweat stains at Great Hall jams
& sang the James Taylor chorus loud & proud
YES, I'M GOING TO CAROLINA IN MY MIND

At Carolina
I met other black folk who were my peers, academically & ambitiously
(an ashamedly rare find in my hometown)
nurturing a newfound black pride & desire
to boldly represent the race &
finally dismantling some old self-doubts that
plagued me for years in integrated schools
casually reinforced by whiteness:
Why was I the only one in this AP course?
This service club?
This honor society?
As an undergrad I saw plenty of examples of black excellence
in the GPAs & leadership experiences of my peers
& in them, I saw myself as an equal & a competitor
providing me with a confidence & pride in my own intelligence & capability
So sometimes when I'm out in the day-to-day, today
discussing my pathway to here
I tell people that I had a black experience at a mostly white college
at this place that made me feel like a citizen of the world
a member of a community

Tar Heel Born
Cedric Brown

& a unique individual
all at the same time

Carolina is where I finally began
the herculean & frightening process of coming out
of the closet of heteronormativity
which requires buttressing one's self against possible & total rejection
in pursuit of a greater
livable
truth

A dear friend noticed a crush I'd developed on the
Zimbabwean grad student who led the campus anti-apartheid efforts
(my sapiosexuality has always been consistent)
Upon sharing my until-then unspoken admission that "yes,
I like guys"
Gina gave me a beautifully empathetic look
head tilted to the side &
hugged me reassuringly

That newly-opened door
grew into a stronger exploration of my homo identity
in the University hothouse
Chaste & unrequited though those years were
By commencement I understood I needed a different ecosystem
if I was indeed going to fully bloom
instead of wilting on the home vine

At Carolina
this scholastic mecca
my personal Kitty Hawk
I tested out these wings
before launching into larger possibilities
but I never forget
where my leaping feet
first left the ground

Tar Heel Born
Cedric Brown

VI.
ESSE QUAM VIDERI:
TO BE, RATHER THAN TO SEEM

Tar Heel Born
Cedric Brown

The paradox of my North Carolina is that
the good & the ugly reside in one place
Politically, a purple tide
making solid progress for awhile & then
retreating, regressing

Ebbing

For my 40th birthday I decided to celebrate with my family
Mommy, sisters, brothers, nieces & nephew
For the first time, I rented a vacation home
on the island haven of Kure Beach
20 minutes south of Wilmington
As my brothers & I drove into town from the airport
(again, for the first time)
we spotted a pickup truck flying huge
Confederate flags on two posts
with skulls-and-crossbones splayed across the flags
& I wondered "what the HELL have I gotten my family into?"
recognizing that the stars-and-bars are a probable sign of
questionable racial justice politics
(at best)
Old ways still haunt
An aging but significant population of folks
still remember Jim Crow
as a lived experience
Still remember Jesse Helms
loved or hated but ever-divisive
Still remember the tension & awkwardness of school busing
creating unspoken lines rarely crossed in classrooms & cliques

& some of the old ways have mutated into
new, coded forms of oppression
rooted in the same dehumanizing DNA

Tar Heel Born
Cedric Brown

Flowing

Later at the beach
as Mommy & I took an evening stroll
we came across a scruffy whiteman in cutoff jeans
& nothing else
watching over his fishing rod posted deep in the sand &
cast into the surf
He too took note of us & fixed his mouth to say
as we passed within acknowledgement distance of one another
"Nice evenin'. How y'all doing?"
Frankly, I was shocked
& then I felt guilty for prejudging him
Thankful that Mommy
in her poised ever-graciousness
replied back to the fisherman
"Fine, thanks. And you?"

Hope springs eternal

Moral Mondays draws a coalition of progressives
from a cross-section of backgrounds
pressing for positive change & equity for all people
My extended family has openly embraced my hubby
without blinking or churchified rhetoric

Both examples lead me to think that
yes, North Carolina can & tries
to love me back
If I love her for who she is
while remembering who I am
in the hopes that someday
we can live together again
in an unthinking, perfect peace

Tar Heel Born
Cedric Brown

I both agree & disagree with Mr. Thomas Wolfe
one of our most cherished Tar Heel writers:
I hope I'm always able to go home again
Back to family
but not to childhood dynamics
Back to places in the country
but not youthful dreams of glory & fame
Back to a combination of the everlasting
& the changes
Back to the familiar
but evolved
In looking homeward
I simultaneously get grounded in where I started
& measure how far I've come
from the boy in UNC pajamas
who sought to sample the world's smorgasbord but
(in the true nature of introverts)
ultimately wants to come back to the comforts & safety of
home

Tar Heel Born
Cedric Brown

VII.
REPRISE

Tar Heel Born
Cedric Brown

North Carolina is my mother
She who birthed & raised me
taught me from her own experiences with segregation
that good must overcome & that everyone deserves a chance
She showed me
how to balance reserve & boldness when making decisions
that work is the stepping stone to success
how to take pride in my appearance & behavior
She insisted on
my believing in the benevolence of a bigger power
being properly respectful & hospitable to people both
familiar & unfamiliar to me
& how to reserve judgment while building greater empathy
She plied me with stick-to-your-ribs comfort food &
nourished a living love of family through knowing the roots
& appreciating the leaves
She instilled in me a gentle gracefulness & a fighting spirit
North Carolina, my mother
& this is why I love her

March 2015
Oakland, California

Tar Heel Born
Cedric Brown

BONUS POEM

OBAMANON:
Living the Obama Phenomenon

Tar Heel Born
Cedric Brown

for jasmin, daveon, zoë, mark, rita, ella, miles, & anna
(& later sydney & zach, who were not yet born)

January 20, 2009

my dears
i wanted to write something to capture the feeling of this day,
of the change that just happened in this country & world
giving me & millions of others
hope & confidence that the days ahead of us
the days that you'll see as a growing child
will put us back on track to peace & prosperity

you see, for the past eight years
some might say 15
some might say 30
we've been on a terribly uncomfortable & unstable path
amidst a longer & bigger history
there was a controversial election
where black people were blocked from voting & there were
serious questions about how the eventual-president
came into office

& then tragedy struck
an attack on American soil
that we never could've imagined
& two towers
symbols of the New York skyline
were destroyed
launching days of deep fear
fear of flying
of talking
of foreigners
of thinking
wondering what had brought on the tragedy
anything less than America-the-perfect
became an unacceptable answer

this was followed by another very unpopular, very contested
invasion
one which in the weeks & days prior
millions of people around the globe
took to the streets to say NO
NO MORE WAR

but the president
who called himself the Decider
went ahead anyway
with faulty information &
a personal grudge
playing the Decider
with thousands of lives of young people
& Iraqi people in a hopeless situation

later floods came to New Orleans
one of our historic & treasured cities
trapping & discouraging poor people
who had no place to go &
no resources to get there
& the Decider flew over those
starving & raggedy masses in his presidential airplane
& looked down on them while the
suffering continued
& the whole world watched & thought
"America can't
or won't
take care of her own people
especially if they're black &
poor"

Tar Heel Born
Cedric Brown

the Decider blinked & did nothing
his TV allies turned the blame around
to wonder openly & aloud on the airwaves
if it was the poor people's fault
for not leaving
(even though they had no transportation &
no credit)
for bringing on the havoc themselves

these are just some of the examples
of the confusion & anger
& heartache & fear
that was cast on our country
which was looking ever so crippled
by greed & lies
money & power & religious control
of our fear

out of all this
in 2004 we heard a new voice on the national scene
one belonging to a funny sounding name & a boyish face
speaking to us about hope
he soon became the only
African American in the US Senate
representing the land of Lincoln
& later we started to pay more attention to this man &
this voice
as we got to know his story
we were mesmerized
son of a single mother, white
born in Hawai'i, our 50th state
dad was a Kenyan international student, black

Tar Heel Born
Cedric Brown

raised as a child in Indonesia
came back to Hawai'i, moving into teenhood
riding waves
playing hoops
& finding his way as a black man
went to college
got serious about service
(a lesson largely learned from mom)
was further schooled on the tough streets of South Side Chicago
& in the hallowed halls of Harvard Law School
came back to Chi-town
got married, went to work
started a family, ran for local office
lost, but came back
because he knew that we could do better
& we the people deserved better
when trying to form a more perfect union
establish justice &
ensure domestic tranquility

when he decided in 2007
as a US Senator
to run for the highest office in the land
i, & many others, was
mildly interested
but wondered how this man
with an odd name & boyish face
would win over a country that was far too comfortable
looking past
& overlooking
considerable black talent:
the honorable Shirley Chisholm
(the first sista to run for president)
the Reverend Jesse Jackson &
some might argue
General Colin Powell & Rev. Al Sharpton
those who trod in the path before him

Tar Heel Born
Cedric Brown

we wondered
can this brotha win?
can he speak to the masses?
can he attract one group
without repelling the other
(which seems to be the nature
of US politics)
does he have a vision?
does he have the skills?
does he have the guts?

besides
the experts had already picked out the Democratic
frontrunner, former first lady,
now-Senator from the most populous eastern state
powerful & worthy in her own right

it became a race to shatter one of many
glass ceilings
around the country club of presidential hopes:
color, gender, religion, orientation

but the brotha said "oh no
i'm going to break up this
pattern of bush, clinton, bush, clinton"
& people started to listen to what
he had to say & examined the
content of his character
& on a cold January day in Iowa
possibilities crystallized like
the snowflakes outside
when the largely-white state said
"yes" to the brotha
which made all of us STOP
& TAKE NOTICE
& think that maybe

Tar Heel Born
Cedric Brown

maybe
hope had room to grow

then South Carolina said yes &
Alabama said yes
& Colorado & Connecticut & Delaware & Georgia
& Nevada & Alaska & so on
& DC said yes
& Virginia & Maryland said yes
& so on & so on
& North Carolina & Hawai'i & Illinois said yes
& so on & so on

the campaign was hard & serious & expensive
hope & change
was the message that carried on as people
got on board

I was in a Washington DC hotel room when a famous journalist,
Tim Russert
who didn't live to see the end of the campaign
said "Ladies & Gentlemen
this is it, we have our
Democratic nominee"

& the numbers confirmed our hopes

before a crowd of 80,000 people
in an open-air Denver stadium
he accepted the nomination
& the challenge

the real work began
convincing a fear-driven &
increasingly weakened nation
that he should be the one to serve
& lead us forward
so he got to work &
we got to work
shaking hands
ringing doorbells
talking to neighbors
raising money
registering voters
spreading hope
overcoming distortions & lies
that wouldn't die
(& somehow never do)
"he's Arabic!"
"he's a muslim!"
"he's a socialist!"
"he's inexperienced!"
"he's too black!"
"he's too radical!"
"he pals around with terrorists!"

he kept cool
kept explaining
kept restating
kept his composure
kept moving
kept meeting
kept hope alive

energized by the possibilities for all of us
under his leadership
we chipped in perhaps like never before

Tar Heel Born
Cedric Brown

black
white
asian
latino
native
jewish
christian
muslim
gay
straight
married
single
& every combination & every other

biting nails &
saying prayers &
emailing neighbors &
giving 25 more dollars &
wearing buttons &
hanging posters &
standing in the line to vote &
making sure others voted &
biting nails &
saying prayers

by 11pm eastern time on
election day night
we knew
"yes we can"
became
(for the moment)
yes we did!
& we did cry
& we did holler
& we did text our mothers
& we did shout praise & thanks
& the world celebrated with us

Tar Heel Born
Cedric Brown

as we recognized the huge significance
of what 65 million of us
from blue states & purple counties
had just accomplished
OUR FIRST BLACK PRESIDENT
& where else would this be possible
but in our country, America
which we could be proud of again
& wear red white blue
& sing O Beautiful for spacious skies
& fly Old Glory without second thoughts

so on this day, January 20, 2009
i hope you understand our huge pride
when Barack Hussein Obama
overcoming all odds
stood on the Capitol steps &
pledged, with his hand on Abraham Lincoln's bible,
to uphold the Constitution
to be the leader of all Americans.

in these most trying times,
we must chip in again, in the ways we can, to
strengthen this nation
to let America be America again
& for the first time
a land of the free & home of the brave
a good neighbor to the world & shepherd of its own

all this means that,
for you,
the possibilities have just been expanded
& even though there are more glass ceilings to break
big goals to accomplish
i really hope you'll do
everything in your power
& God's power to be

Tar Heel Born
Cedric Brown

all you can be
we worked this hard for you
these doors are opened for you!
& i don't have to be skeptical
when i say
you can be what you want to
be in life
yes you can
yes we can
yes, we
can
YES!

With love,
Uncle Cedric

Tar Heel Born
Cedric Brown

www.ingramcontent.com/pod-product-compliance
Lightning Source LLC
Chambersburg PA
CBHW052030290426
44112CB00014B/2448